Survivors
by L.A. Ross

Survivors
by L. A. Ross

L. A. Ross
P. O. Box 246
Oswego, IL 60543
laross.0904@gmail.com
website: laross.info

Copyright ©1987- 2018 by Leslie Aileen Ross

All rights reserved.

"Survivors" is fully protected under the copyright laws of the United States of America, the British Commonwealth, including Canada, and all other countries of the Copyright Union. All rights, including professional, amateur, motion picture, recitation, lecturing, public reading, radio broadcasting, television, web, digital, and the rights of translation into foreign languages are strictly reserved.

This purchased play does not include performance rights; however, actresses may use portions of this script for auditions.

Request performance rights to "Survivors" from:
 L.A. Ross
 P. O. Box 246
 Oswego, IL 60543-8044
 Or laross.0904@gmail.com

Please request performance rights at least 8 weeks before performance.

Cover art: Copyright 2018 by Leslie Aileen Ross

Dedication
To all survivors and the people who support them.

Acknowledgments

"Survivors" was revised at the Feminist Women's Writing Workshops (FW3) of July 1987 and 1989, had its first staged reading in April 1989 by the International Society of Dramatists (directed by Alex Rubin), was a finalist in the New Playwrights Competition of The Ann White Theatre, was a semifinalist in the Siena College Playwrights' Competition, had two staged readings in 1992, and was further developed through the play development program at The Playwrights' Center, Chicago.

The playwright would like to thank playwrights and mentors Steve Carter, Kathleen Thompson, and Anne McGravie for their support and comments on this and other plays. Special thanks, too, to the women at FW3 and other writers and support people including Barb, Cathy and Jeff, Diana, Di, Julie, Kenna, Linda, Mary, Nancy, Vickie, and Yo.

First production and words of thanks

This play was improved through a play development program by The Playwrights' Center, Chicago, in 1992. Special thanks to: Ed Sobel, director of play development, who guided the collaboration between the director and playwright; George Tafelski, director, who had a vision for this play (when few others would touch it) and gently guided the play, playwright, and performance to realization; Jane Dillingham, assistant director, the director's right arm; Kimberly Furst, Billie 3, who brought love and freedom to Billie; Christina Koehlinger, Billie 2, who brought the innocent child to life; and Dado, Billie, who brought the Billie's together.

Music for the original production was written by George Sawyn.

Characters

Billie -- a very angry woman in her mid-30s

Billie 2 -- Billie as a child

Billie 3 -- the part of Billie who loves love and music

Time and Place

1986 -- therapist's office (Chicago) and Billie's mind

Notes:

The set may be sparse or a more designed. The stage may have an area for each part of Billie. Props may be used, if desired.

As the play progresses, the Billies move closer and closer together until, at the end, they are "integrated" into Billie.

Once in a while, the playwright has entered a line that is three asterisks, which denotes a longer passage of time (beats). The actresses and/or director may decide to make the pauses uncomfortably long in some cases and shorter in others.

Multimedia Presentation

The playwright also envisions the possibility of using two or more slide projectors during the play. At first, slides of a man and a man's things appear for a few seconds. As the play progresses, the slides are up longer and longer until the man can be identified. Slides may include: Old Spice, shoe polish, hair oil, a man's hairy arms, a man's hairy chest, and get as explicit as the theater cares to. The images should get sharper, clearer, and more explicit as the play progresses.

Throughout the play, perhaps in the blackouts, a man's voice can call Billie's name. Location of the voice should vary.

Scents (like Old Spice) could waft throughout the theater at times.

(Stage: low light. Billie is sitting on a chair, center stage.)

Billie *(muffled):* No!

(more clearly)

No! Go away!

(standing, moving toward a coat rack)

Leave me alone!

Damn!

Shit! I'm yelling at a coat rack.

What's going on?

I think I'm going crazy.

Billie 2: O-ma and O-pa live in Florida. Little green lizards climb on the screen of the porch. Wild parakeets fly free -- all the pretty colors. Will all land on the parakeet tree at 7:00, every night.

I walk down to the pond, by the banana plant. O-pa's bananas are the smallest, sweetest bananas I've ever seen.

It's early morning and a fog hugs the air over the pond like a cloud. I wonder what it would be like to walk through the fog, the mist, a cloud.

(Pause.)

I lie on the grass and see pictures in the clouds. It looks like cotton candy. White cotton candy. I love the way the cotton candy turns to water in my mouth. It disappears. Turns to sweet water.

Billie: Yeah, white and water have always intrigued me. Maybe that's why they sent me to Florida.

They said it was an eighth-grade graduation present. Some present. Maybe they were getting back at me for the presents I gave them.

Billie 2: Daddy, here's *your* Christmas present. I hope you like it. We saved up for it for a long time.

Billie: We had saved up our money for ages. All of us kids put our money together to get that bird. Could it only have been four or five dollars? It seems like that's all it was but, 20 or 30 years ago, it was a lot of money for kids.

God, he hated that bird.

I should have known what he wanted for Christmas I was the oldest and, therefore, responsible for all. So, under the guise of a magnanimous gift, he shipped me off to Florida to spend the summer with his parents.

O-pa, Wilhelmis L. the first, always made breakfast while he fought with his wife.

Wilhelmis L. the first. I always wondered: The first what? W.L.'s first son was the second and the second's son's first son was the third.

They say people who name their children after themselves are 90 percent more likely to abuse those children than people who name their children more creatively.

My brothers called my father Wee Willy and Willy Wonka Wonka.

O-pa and O-ma fought in Dutch -- screaming and yelling at each other in that horrible throat-clearing language. The language is so ... They can even make whipped cream sound disgusting. Who'd put *slagroom* on pumpkin pie? Who'd call a loved one a *lieverd*?

I know where my father's anger started.

When the screaming began,

Billie 2: I walked outside to watch the dewdrops form on the Cadillac window.

I play with the drops -- pushing them together. I try to get a droplet big enough to roll down the window. I draw faint lines with my finger, making a path for the drop so it can scoot down.

I love to move the droplets together and watch them take their own course, joining other streams of rolling drops. Streams rolling into rivers, rolling into the ocean.

Billie: God, I hated to fish. Every morning, we got up early so we could eat and be on the dock by 5:00 am. I never understood why we had to go so early but we did.

O-ma liked flounder so she was always yelling, in Dutch, of course, to fish on the bottom. You catch all sorts of ugly creatures when you drag your hook across the bottom of the ocean -- conks, sea bass, scavengers, pilot fish. If you catch one those babies, you know

Billie 2: sharks are close by.

Billie: Sharks are always close by. Sharks and scavengers. The sharks go looking for meat.

Scavengers clean up the leftovers. Eat the remains in the losers of the survival of the fittest. Feast on the weak. Fishers look down on the scavengers. If you catch one, you certainly don't eat it. O-ma told me they have bad meat that only the poor people eat.

Billie 2: But, they do something none of the other fishes do -- clean up the ocean -- kind of the garbage collectors of the sea. Cleaning it up, making it healthy and beautiful for the other fishes.

Billie: Sea bass are among the ugliest fish I've ever seen. I caught one of those ugly, flat-bottomed fish and thought I'd catch the warts on its body. When you look at it head on, it's almost shaped like a long triangle. I'd play with my line hoping it would, miraculously, fall off the hook. Even with a cloth from O-pa's fishing cart, I didn't want to touch the thing.

I remember a picture of me holding two mackerel -- mack-crel O-ma called them.

So, it's all my fault.

Billie 2: All my fault 'cause I'm the oldest and should have known better.

Billie: Funny how the mind wanders. I hadn't thought about that summer for a long time. Both grandparents are dead now. All gone. Like they never existed.

(Pause.)

I used to play piano ... and violin, viola, 'cello. Started college as a music major. But I just got too angry. Had to change my major to save my sanity.

Billie 3: Years ago, I played a concert at a religious grade school. Between preconcert warm-up and the concert, I wandered around the halls. One bulletin board had each child's picture as the head of a flower. A light rain was falling.

The text above the flowers said, "God rains on all his flowers." I looked at that board and wondered if it meant all God's children need rain to grow. And then I decided God's children also need sunshine to grow. I wonder what the designer meant. The more I thought about it, the more confused I got. Cacti live without much rain and tropical plants live with excessive rain. What's that supposed to mean? Some people are designed to deal with more rain than others? I burn out my brain. Yes, Ms. King, "there's just too much rain falling..."

Billie: Too much rain. Too much pain. No pain. No gain. I'm confused.

I am surprised, for example, at my inability to describe my headaches to my doctor. The strangest headaches I've ever had. Starts in my left shoulder, goes up my neck to the back of my head, and then travels around the left side of my brain to my forehead.

"What kind of pain?"

Billie 2: Pain. You know. Ouch. Hurts.

Billie: "Is it a sharp, stabbing pain or a dull, constant ache?"

Billie 2: I don't remember but ...

I don't know.

Billie: "Well, how do you know it's pain?"

In the strictly philosophical sense, I don't know how I know. At some point in my past someone told me what I'm feeling is pain. Perhaps they lied to me. Perhaps it has another name. I misinterpreted the doctor's question, so he tells me.

I have always misinterpreted questions -- doctor's questions, test questions, and marriage proposals.

I also misinterpret morning fog.

Billie 3: Morning fog. Early morning fog. Look at the sunrise. Concentrate on the brilliance. Think of the wakeup call to nature. Watch the red-orange glowing in the east. See the orange glow dissipate the fog -- burning it off so a new day is washed, then dried. A naked day, sun dried; a promise to all of us.

Billie: Yeah, I wish I could think that way and believe it.

They've given up on me. Too tough a nut to crack. My friends have given me up to professionals who repeat phrases and try classic "techniques." When I recognize the techniques -- I read too much -- I think they are inauthentic.

Authenticity is very important to me. Everyone says, "How ya' doin'?", which, in rough translation means "I see you." Stupid me. I always answer.

My brother would say, you can say anything when you're smiling. Smile, nod your head up and down, and say, "Fuck you, very much" to the next person you see. They'll smile back! Always do.

I smile when my boss pays me a compliment. I know it doesn't mean anything but I play the game. He doesn't matter to me. I separate him from my life. Other people, too. But the result is the same. The people you love don't want to love you. The people who love you aren't the people you want to love. You can't make people feel something they don't feel.

My part-time orchestras are more important to me than writing articles for "Sanitation Engineering," a trade magazine that prides itself on being on top of the portable outhouse industry. I mean, how much can you say about shit? Month after month you write about the "innovations" of sanitation engineering. When I interviewed for the job, I thought the magazine was a satirical publication -- that "Sanitation Engineering" was a spoof on the industry. At the time, I had no other offers and needed some money so I took it. Never expected to spend a decade here.

Still, I try to do good work. I used to get lectures from a friend about this -- before she gave up on me. "Your expectations are too high. It's insane," she said, "to think anyone at work cares about you or the work. They don't want to be at work any more than you do.

They, too, turn writing about shit into mortgage payments. They don't want to admit *they* work for "Sanitation Engineering." They certainly don't want to talk shop at a party." Why haven't I learned my lesson? Why do they keep changing the rules?

"Well," she said, "see a shrink. She can teach you techniques to handle these *situations*." Techniques to handle situations. We've been dehumanized again and are taught to dehumanize others. Management techniques. Techniques we got. Compassion "have we none. And, yet, I will be ha-a-a-a-apy. Hey, hoe. Nobody home."

Nobody home.

Alice doesn't live here anymore.

"Life isn't like the movies," she said. I know enough to wish it were. No one shits in the movies. No one cries alone. No one dies alone. Someone always happens to hear the dying person's last words. Someone always wrings the excess water from a cool compress and wraps the sick person's head. Someone always hugs the unlovable. It all comes out in the end. In the movies.

Books, too. A woman enlists in the Confederate army and fools all the men-folk.

Billie 3: She rides a horse better than any man and she loves the excitement of war.

Billie: And I, being so pragmatic, wonder what she did when she had her period. They didn't have tampons back then.

Did the author do complete research? Or did she think that little point too *too* to put into the book? The woman warrior gets up early to pee and wash. But supplies were short. Wouldn't someone get suspicious of a man collecting cotton for his own use? When I was in Russia, I was told the women use cotton and a little board. Were they teasing me?

But, somehow, I forget these details and get involved in the stories.

Billie 2: I cry.

Billie 3: I cry at the sad parts. I cry at the happy parts. I cry when people get married.

Billie: I cry because I know my life will never be one tenth as lovely or beautiful as other people's lives. I cry during the war movies when one soldier holds another as he dies because I know ... I know

Billie 2: no one will hold me.

Billie: I will die alone.

(Pause.)

"Life isn't like the movies," they tell me. My life hasn't been scripted.

(Pause.)

My father's believed his script was the Bible.

Billie 2: "Ye shall love one another."

Billie: And he certainly did. He tried to have sex with everyone. He's been discovered in bed with girls and boys and rubber toys.

Games. Someone always got hurt in his games. We'd play screwdriver toss. He'd throw it and you catch it with your body -- back, shoulder, head, arm, leg. Or, he'd stick a pencil in the kid to see if it's done. Let me tell you, lead stays in your skin for years. It still shows, 30 odd years later.

It's more than pencil lead that is embedded in my skin.

I went downtown to watch this woman perform. I've seen her before. Actually, we've even had a few meals together.

Billie 3: Yes, so. So, she is beautiful. She's one of those people people see on stage and fall in love with. Light laughter, easy going, and a voice just breaking into maturity. A voice sure and solid. Supported. Strength. The way she closes her eyes and sings with the bass it's almost embarrassing. I imagine the voices in bed together. How do they move together so exactly with their eyes closed? How can they see where to put the notes? Talent. I could listen forever. She tosses her head with just the right amount of playfulness -- no one could mistake it for egotism. Playful innocence. That's how it comes off.

Billie: I know better.

Billie 3: Every time she sings, I fall a little bit in love.

The songs are so right, so moving that, even in the Chicago summer humidity in a sweltering bar, the hairs on my arm rise up, prickling my skin.

Billie: It's silly.

You want to know everyone I've fallen in love with? They are all inapproachable: this singer (a long time ago), an English teacher, a 'cellist, a philosophy major, an alcoholic guitar player, a Chicago playwright,

Billie 3: Cagney *and* Lacy, Annie Hall, Richard Dreyfuss, Steve Goodman, and I'm sure there were others.

Billie: When real people couldn't love me back, I turned to performers.

Billie 3: I've heard things -- sounds, words, music -- so beautiful, tears have wandered down my face. Tears move more slowly when they fall from beauty instead of sadness.

I had always thought that 'cellist in music school was a bit strange when he talked about music that made him cry.

After studying music for most of my life I never had that experience until we played the "Concerto for Piano and Orchestra in G" by Maurice Ravel. As the soloist played, the tears meandered down my face and left salt streaks on my viola. I forgot to play my part. I just wanted to listen to her play the piano. The fast parts were . . . I can't describe the feeling. The slow passages were so melodic, beautiful, soothing, like a gentle lover come to comfort and stroke ...

so beautiful, so moving, so ...

Billie: Damn --

Billie 3: words just aren't enough.

Billie: It's stupid. Sittin' around playing music by a bunch of dead white men. Playing your heart out for some conductor's ego. This pitiful orchestra prepares "Stars and Stripes Forever" as an encore. Some old wannbe band director couldn't find a marching band so we play band music. I don't have time to live out someone else's dreams.

Billie 3: I dream and dream. Sometimes they are the most wonderful dreams. Dreams like scenes from classic movies. A knock on the door when you need someone to talk to. A hug from a friend when bad news has found its way to your personal door step. A lover to turn to when work is just too, too demanding. A lover to wake to and cuddle all Saturday morning. A lover you won't leave the bed for. A lover who is gentle and good and caring.

A lover. A lover whose touch becomes firm;

Billie: then demanding. A lover's touch becomes rough. The lover's face turns ugly. The lover's breath smells like barf. No, that's mine. Forcibly mingled with that man's mind. Teeth bite each other. Repulsion. Anger. Fear. Pain. Violence.

I wake up crying. Screaming. Angry. I want to beat someone up. But he's gone. Goddamn him. When I'm finally big enough, angry enough ... he's gone.

Faces of lovers always turn into his face. The face of a madman. An ugly, uncontrollable mad man. Fuck him. Why can't he leave me alone?

So, are you going to help me?

OK. So, are you going to help me help me? My friends have given up.

They are too busy for "such foolishness." Too busy for anger. Too busy for pain. Too busy for childish behavior. Only mature people, people who don't feel pain, are allowed.

I need to talk to someone.

I need to talk.

God, I need

Billie 3: to talk to her.

Billie: Except now I know I can fool her with a laugh and a light lilt to my voice.

Billie 3: I've made friends with a performer.

Billie: I've studied how it's done. I can deceive her: the person I thought was undeceivable. Ha.

Now that I know I can deceive her, I don't need her. I don't need her.

Billie and Billie 2: My needs don't matter.

Billie: I want someone ... someone to care about; to care about me. No more illusions. No more fantasies.

Billie 3: I've fallen in love again. She's tall and slender and blond and green-eyed and brilliant and low-voiced and has expressive hands.

Billie: And is also unobtainable.

Billie 3: When she steps up onto the podium and lifts her baton, all minds meet her supreme knowledge. It glimmers -- a diamond in a pit of a small, community orchestra. She tells the 'celli and basses to play closer to the bridge and asks the brass to use less tongue. My mind wanders. I wonder what her lover would do if he/she were hearing this phrase: Use less tongue.

I dream her long, out-reaching fingers massage my back and shoulders and then my neck. Her hands, while not leaving my neck, direct me, with pressure and kindness, backwards, until she turns up my chin and holds the back of my head as her lips move into mine. I touch her beautiful hair and yearn for more.

> *(Offstage: the sound of someone pounding on a door or a body slamming into something.)*

Billie 2: I open the door and go outside. It's a perfect 70 degree day. The smell of spring just turning to summer. The sheets are hung up to dry.

Billie 3: A fresh, 100 percent cotton shirt on my naked chest excites me. The sound of rubbing cotton. The coarse fabric being masturbated by fabric touching fabric -- the tiny groan the fabric makes when it changes directions, changes directions, changes directions. Unbutton each button slowly, deliberately, from the top down. Linger beneath the cotton like a young lover. See my breasts for the first time. Feel them. Touch them. Taste them. Nurse. I will cradle your head and protect you, hon, child, from the stresses of today's world. Let me stroke you as you suck, my little one. Yes, play with the other as you suck. Fondle it. Open your wide eyes and see it as you've never seen it before. Notice its texture. Note the little raspberry on top. Press it. Feel les jeunes petits pois. Hug me like a child hugs a teddy. Roll us over. Let me lie above you and lower my breast into your mouth no handed. Let me press your head to my chest. Too much tongue. Light strokes. Flickering tongue. Suck and tongue and press and move and press and roll. Oh, my God.

Billie 2 and 3: Oh, my

Billie: God.

Billie and Billie 3: Look what

Billie, Billie 2, and Billie 3: I've told you!

Billie: God. I'm just like him. I'm a sex maniac. I hate that. I hate him. I hate me.

Billie 2: I'm bad.

Billie: I'm obscene.

I watch people. Thinking about them -- what they would look like.

I watched her bite at a hang nail. Suddenly, it dawned on me that that is what she would look like beneath her husband. The private, semi-painful look. Slightly mischievous. The look her husband looks for. The look that lets him know she is ready. I was embarrassed I noticed.

I recognize that expression. I hate to admit it. Sex gets in the way.

A guy I once dated told me I "was reasonably attractive." Now, what does that mean? I was supposed to find that somehow reassuring?

He also told me he wanted "sex frequently and with variety." I told him go find Variety -- that I hoped she would satisfy him.

Quite frankly, I find sex repulsive; that's why I'm so confused. Fantasy is fine but having someone really touch me is something else.

You think I need help, don't you? You think it will get worse and worse and I'll end up killing myself, don't you? Don't turn it around on me! I'm alone because all my friends are gone. But I don't need help.

Billie 2 *(softly)*: Help. Please help me.

Billie: How can they do it? These women. Those women. The women who've been raped. How can they ever sleep with a man again?

Me?

(Pause.)

I still like the fall ...

Billie 2: The leaves are so beautiful in the fall. Golden sunsets glowing above the pumpkin, apple cider, squash. Peaceful. Cool.

Billie: but I hate summer. I hate summer? My Grandma, my good Grandma, died in the summer.

My grandmother used to carry bottles of shoe polish around the nursing home saying, "This oughta do it." When she died, they found a razor blade in her toothpaste. That oughta do it, too.

I carry bottles of wine around saying, "This oughta do it." Only I'm talking about a cure for insomnia. Although Grandma's cure for life would work quite effectively.

Billie 2: My good grandma used to let me sleep with her. Her bed was safe and warm. I used to love waking up on those lazy mornings. The sunlight sneaking through the blinds, waking me up,

Billie 3: waking us up, striping our bodies. The sun spreading the warmth, the warmth of a body in bed next to me. Arms that could cradle my shoulders for hours; a waterbed encourages slow motions. Each movement rocks, imitates the womb and childhood rooms and floating on a raft, drifting down a river on a slow -- moving Sunday afternoon. Pretending he loves me

Billie 2 and Billie 3: and will protect me like Pa in *Little House on the Prairie*,

Billie 3: pretending my life is under the control of a magnificent, benevolent, caring, kind man; pretending that nothing --

Billie (*in a "yeah, dream on" way*): not earthquake, death, famine, tornadoes, the earth's end --

Billie 3: can diminish this loving, caring feeling. Pretending we can do this forever. Afraid to move, afraid to go to the bathroom, because, once disturbed, it will never be this way again.

Billie and Billie 3: I love(d) leading the double life.

Billie 3: Dropping him off at the train station

Billie: like a dutiful wife

Billie 3: and going to work where they think the only thing my *friend* and I share is a few meals on the weekend.

Billie: Even though sex was not an actuality -- even though our relationship consisted only of repeated foreplay -- even so,

Billie 3: I feel wickedly good about finally leading an adult life.

Billie: I felt more adult not telling anyone about anything.

Billie 3: A few people know his name.

Billie: No one knows we slept together

Billie 3: and share the same air that surrounds the bed.

Or that we shower together, lathering each other's bodies with scented soaps, fearful, still, of each other's privacy. No one knows how difficult it is to leave the warmth on Monday mornings, to give him up to the train station and to go to work (only moderately late) pretending to lead a boring, single life.

Billie: No, no sex. Why? Don't want to make babies. Pill? High blood pressure. No. Excuses every one. I don't ... I don't ... I don't like to be touched ... 1 don't like to be touched below...

(Pause.)

My friends are quite ready to believe I am "just depressed" or "have a chemical imbalance." But they don't seem to like the truth very much.

They are all going away. They are frightened by my illness. Or tired of my complaints.

They try to argue with me about it. I tell them to shut up. I am having a hard enough time with this. I don't have the energy to help them deal with it, too. They want me to say everything is fine. I can't tell them what they want to hear so they argue with me. "You're just depressed," they say.

Billie 2: "Need more exercise."

Billie: "Need more sex!"

Billie 3: "Need a good man!"

Billie: "Need a new job!"

Billie 3: "Need a good woman!"

Billie and Billie 2: I gotta get out of here.

Billie 2: Whenever things get too noisy at the house or someone is acting kinda crazy, I go for a walk. I take lots of walks. Today, I'm going to the zoo. Mom won't mind. She thinks I'm mature for my age. ... I love the sound of the leaves crunching under foot. The sound of shoes on gravel. I stop and look at everything ... the birds singing

(does bird imitations)

"whipper-will" and "bob white!" Good Grandma told me they sing their names. At the zoo, though, there are all sorts of animals to watch. I feel kinda sorry for them -- they have to live in cages. I like to watch them, though.

Billie: I watched the primates for hours. The teats of the females were so unexpectedly pink and sagging. Almost like someone attached fur to a human female. Attached the fur everywhere but her teats. And someone, probably an overzealous lover, had sucked and sucked and pulled and stretched them until they were long and pink and hot from abuse.

The male sat up, proudly, demonstrating his sexuality. He knew he was on display. He said, "I'll give these mothers something to explain. See kiddies? See this wonderful piece? I call it my Big Wally. Let me hold it up for you so you can see it better. Want to hold it? Big Wally likes to be held. Big Wally likes to be stroked. Give me your hand. Come on, do what I say."

Give me your hand? What kind of man does something like that? Men. I hate them. They are all the same. I feel like I'm drowning. They force my face down.

Last night, my roommate found me after hiding behind my couch. I don't know what I was doing there.

Billie 2 (*hiding*): It's safe here. No one can see me. I'm invisible.

Billie: She, so gently coaxed me to come out. I was Venus de Milo -- beyond feeling. My arms were broken off. My roommate cried for me because I couldn't cry for myself. She held me, rocking me, touching me gently, holding me together -- keeping me in one piece. Keeping me from fragmenting.

Billie 3: Body heat connecting, gently warming each other like the sun warming a lizard who recently crawled out of the shade.

Billie 2: I feel safe. Loved.

Billie: I don't remember the rest of the night very well, but she stood or sat right next to me all night   through the shaking ... I got so cold. I felt things happening to me that I knew weren't happening. Someone was driving a stick up ...

She hugged me nearly constantly. I sometimes thought she was the only reason the statue didn't quietly crack and float apart. I saw the little pieces break off and try to start floating away. Just as they started moving, she'd move slowly (not to startle them) but definitely to each piece and firmly push it back where it belonged. I thought of the slapstick routine where drawers of a desk pop out whenever a drawer is closed. My body had seen too many movies. It was doing the same thing. Even as she hugged me, holding all the pieces together, my body shivered with planned fragmentation -- escape.

My father never touched me.

I often wondered why not.

Billie 2: Wasn't I pretty enough?

Billie: He never tried anything with me. Babysitters. Mother's sisters. Old women. Young women. Never me. I know it's kind of strange but that always kind of offended me. Here he was having sex with girls my age and younger and he ignored me.

My brother once told me that my father told one of my boyfriends, John, to "get her drunk and take advantage of her."

John would never have touched me, and, even if he had, he never would have told my father. John was one of those men who is easy to size up. Although he was slow mentally, he was always quick to evaluate another's mood -- kind of like a devoted dog.

He wanted me to marry him. I told him my father had ruined all that. He asked me what I meant. I couldn't say. I just didn't want to be married. Couldn't stand the thought of sex. Couldn't stand the restraint. Ah, Gloria Steinem to the rescue -- "I can't mate in captivity."

I just want some warmth. Any body lying next to you is warm. Some caring. Some warm gentleness. It never lasts long enough. Someone becomes uncomfortable or someone has to pee and it's all undone. You just can't crawl back into bed

Billie 3: and snuggle up in exactly the same way.

Billie: The moment is destroyed. It doesn't

Billie 2: evaporate like dew in the morning sun;

Billie: it is jerked away like a bad dentist tearing out a tooth. It's violent.

No wonder we are all lost.

No, it's never been good.

Billie 2: I leave my body and watch. I float up to the ceiling

Billie: and I watch him hungrily attack the body.

Sometimes I just close my eyes and turn off my mind and wait 'til it's over.

Billie 2 (*praying*): Oh, dear God, make it end quickly.

Billie: No. I can't even pretend. I don't enjoy it. Men frighten me. I fear for my life.

I know all men aren't bad -- only all the men I've known.

Only all men who would be attracted to me.

Something happens. Something always happens. It always happens. Always.

Everything starts out OK.

Billie 3: Slow. Nice. Gentle. No words. No asking.

Billie: But then, something happens. They always get violent. Lose control. They start fucking and it doesn't matter anymore who or what is under them. They get angry and fuck. It always happens.

I have nothing else to say today. Nothing to say. What's really wrong? What if I tell you?

Billie 2: What happens if I tell?

Billie: Will it really matter? I want it to matter to you. I want it to matter to someone. God damn it. I want it to matter to someone.

How astute of you. Yes, I'm angry. I am very angry. Maybe we should talk about it after I smash a few walls down. Why? What do you fuckin' mean? Why don't *you* sit down? You're so condescendingly sweet I'd like to pull your tongue out.

Can I bum a cig?

So, I'm talking to you so maybe I can learn how to save the rest of my friends. How to handle it so they don't have to.

Why can't they handle it? What can't they handle? My anger? My past? My present? My future?

I haven't even told them I think about suicide. Or that, every morning I wake up wishing I were dead. Or that every fuckin' night and often during the day, when the pain is too violent, the hope turns into depression. I don't tell them I chant, "I wish I were dead. I wish I were dead," until I become conscious enough to cry for a while and then move off to the shower. Or until I fall asleep.

And I fall asleep after reading for hours. I wake up around 4:00 am sweating and wishing I were dead. ... Two hours later, I can't get out of bed because I hurt too much and I'm too tired. I don't want to step into the shower and get all wet but I know this is another one of those things that people don't want to do but have to. And, when I finally do get in the shower, the hot water feels good.

Billie 3: The hot water feels so good, while I'm, taking a shower, I don't want to leave. The soap smells great --

Billie 2: it reminds me of a spring rain falling gently.

Billie 3: The hot water massages my aching back and shoulders like a tender lover. And I don't want to get out. I don't want to leave. I want to stay here, where it is

Billie 2 and Billie 3: warm and safe.

Billie: But, after lots more arguing with myself, I get out of the shower.

I get dressed, fix a cup of coffee, and I'm off to work. I bring the coffee with me and drink it in my car -- it's my carrot. As long as the coffee is ahead of me, I keep goin'.

I've fought a few major battles before I get to work. No one knows.

Billie and Billie 2: I've never told anyone.

Billie: Angry? Naw, I'm not angry.

I don't *feel* angry. Yes, maybe I should be angry but what good will that do?

Oh, shit,

Billie and Billie 2: don't make me do that.

Billie: I hate acting. Now, you're going to try to make me angry because you think I should be angry.

I can't get angry. When you get angry, you lose control.

Billie and Billie 2: It's not good to lose control. It's childish to lose control -- immature --

Billie: sick.

Billie 2: People throw things and people get hurt. People hurt people. Hit them. Threaten them. Say things they don't mean

Billie: but can never be taken back. "You can kill people with words, too, you know. You're just like your father when you act like this! Do you want to be like him? You're just like your father."

Billie 2: No! No! No!

Billie: I'm not like that mother fuckin' bastard.

Billie 2: You shut up. You don't know my daddy.

Billie: At church, people saw a polite, God-fearing man. A Sunday school teacher. A youth group director. An Indian Guide father. A Boy Scout leader. A baseball coach. A loving, caring father. A devoted husband.

He needed his supply of little bodies like a vampire needs blood.

He had to keep changing groups so people wouldn't notice the scars he left on young people's throats -- and elsewhere.

If he hadn't studied the sociology of mass movements, he had a God-given gift for collecting the little children unto him. He sized up the children quickly. Knew which ones he could touch; which ones would talk.

He got the babysitters through the church. Young girls who lived on the other side of town. Young girls whose parents dropped them off. Whose parents seemed to let the kids go wild. Young girls who liked to flirt but who probably had only been a tease to boys their own age. Ah, but in the hands of a man -- a well-respected, church-going man -- whatever happened was a gift from the heavens. Given for us to enjoy.

Yeah, I saw him flirt. I heard the stories. I saw things that didn't look quite right but that weren't exactly punishable by law -- not then, anyway.

I intuitively feared for my friends. One Saturday, I came in the house and saw my father lying on the floor next to one of my friends. I didn't know she was coming over. Didn't expect her. I don't know how the scene unfolded. They were asleep together -- or so it appeared. They both had clothes on. It would look innocuous enough if you didn't know my father. Some might have even seen the scene as beautiful. Maybe cute. But I felt strange. My overwhelming desire was to figure out how to get her away from him before he hurt her. I hoped I had not been too late.

Was I too late?

My mother fought a three-month battle for life at the hospital one summer. She fought and won to come back to her children. When she was released from the hospital, that prick refused to pick her up. He had too much work to do. He "worked" seven days a week, and, fortunately, was rarely home.

So, mother took a cab from the hospital some 20 miles away. The cabbie helped her out of the car, into the house and to the couch. He got her suit case and flowers. He, too, heard noises in the back bedroom and held my mother's hand when he noticed the tears. My father had had the babysitter.

We didn't know the whole story for years. But, even though we didn't talk about it, we knew something was wrong with our father. We heard the arguments and the accusations and the denials. We heard the screaming and the yelling and the door slamming and the broken glass and the smacks and the sounds of a body falling into the walls and bookcases and chests and beds.

> *(Offstage: the sound of a body slamming into something.)*

We heard the "No, no -- the kids ... don't."

> *(Billie 2 hides.)*

And the "I don't care about the kids. This is what I want and I want it now."

We heard my mother's pain and my father's anger. And his laughter when she told him he was raping her.

He said, "A husband can't rape his wife. A husband rape his wife. That's a good one!"

> *(Pause.)*

Good times? Do I remember any good times? No. I know I should but I don't remember anything pleasant about the man or the years we lived together as a family.

Every meal was a battleground. Every holiday a major war. I hated to see him. My brothers and I hoped he would go out of town even more often. We'd pretend to be sick to stay away from the dinner table when he was home.

Yes, I hate him. I hate that fucking asshole.

Billie and Billie 2: What can I do? He's my father/daddy.

Billie: I've awakened in the middle of the night smelling a smell I could never identify. I had the feeling it was evil. It was anger -- unlike any other smell. For years, I've asked people to identify it.

I thought I was going crazy. No one else ever smelled it. But, I continued to wonder what it was. It reminded me of a reoccurring nightmare I had as a child. It always started with a vague yet comfortable feeling.

Billie 2 *(drawing)*: I make pictures of my dreams. Friendly lines greet me. Hold me. It is so kind, so reassuring, so relaxing. Then, all of a sudden, the lines start moving faster and faster and I become more and more afraid. The lines get angrier and angrier and I become more and more frightened until I wake up yelling.

Billie: And the nightmare reoccurred and reoccurred and I couldn't figure out what it meant. But it frightened me even when I was awake.

Billie 2: I was afraid to fall asleep because the lines would get me.

Billie and Billie 2: They always fooled me with their kindness in the beginning but they always got violent.

I wake up. Afraid to scream out.

Billie 2: I flip the pillow over. If I flip the pillow over, I bury the badness. I hug my stuffed dog and pray that the lines won't get me.

Billie: Well, the other day, while I was brushing my teeth and it suddenly dawned on me that the smell is the smell of dried blood. Dried blood. Don't ask me how I came to that conclusion. I just suddenly felt that it was right. Dried blood.

(Pause.)

Billie and Billie 3: A love of music.

Billie 3: Yes, despite it all,

Billie and Billie 3: I still love music.

Billie: It's been with me longer than anything.

Billie 3: And I love love. I want to be close to someone.

Billie: I need someone to show a little interest. Someone to whom I can say,

Billie, Billie 2, and Billie 3: *(Each Billie says "Hold me," separately, but in rapid succession.)*

Hold me, hold me, hold me.

Billie: Hold me 'til I say it's enough.

Billie 3: Hold me. Shhh, don't talk

Billie: to me. Don't think about sex. Just touch me.

Billie 2: Hold me.

Billie 3: Softly

Billie and Billie 2: tell me everything is going to be all right.

Billie, Billie 2, and Billie 3: Hold me.

Billie: Hold me -- together.

Billie: Strange pain in my head, again. It feels like someone is trying to split my brain in half like a nutcracker splitting a walnut. The nut cracks exactly on the seam. The pain is sharp but doesn't last long.

I am exhausted. I can't sleep. The pain-drains my body of-energy-just-like a-vampire-drains-his-victim's-body-of-blood. My eyes stare at the ceiling. I don't care that I'm not sleeping. The pain is going away.

Why can't it all go away? Why can't I feel good again? I don't want to deal with it.

I'm supposed to talk about it when I don't want to talk about it. But then, when I want to talk about it, no one wants to listen.

Everyone is going away. I'm not asking you, or anyone, to pull me up by yourself. I'm just asking for help.

And you dare tell me not to consider suicide. You dare tell me to call you first. What are you going to do? Tell me you'll call me a week from now when you have time?

And what's with you? All this good, good, good. Get your anger out. I'll give you get your anger out! How would you like to see that ashtray go flying through the window? Followed by this fuckin' chair and, while I'm at it, you!

What are you staring at? You goin ta' start ballin'. "Cry, baby, cry."

> *(Billie raises are hand as if she is going to strike someone.)*

Stop that crying or I'll give you something to cry about!

> *(Pause.)*

I'm sorry. I didn't mean to frighten you. I didn't mean to touch you. I'm sorry. I've failed. I've lost my temper. I'm bad. I lost control. Are you going to kill me now?

> *(Pause.)*

Oh, dear Jesus, I'm sorry.

Billie and Billie 2: I didn't mean to. I feel so bad.

Billie: Mother was right.

Billie and Billie 2: I'm just like him. I lost it. I lost my temper. I'm bad.

Billie 2: I'm afraid.

Billie 3: I'm afraid I'll miss it. Miss something beautiful. Because

Billie, Billie 2, and Billie 3: I'm afraid.

Billie: Afraid I'll get pregnant.

OK. It's an excuse.

It's dirty. Vulgar.

What is? You know. The whole thing. The touching. The poking. Prodding. Passion explodes into violence. Always. Violence frightens me. Men can't control it. It explodes within them. They have to hurt. All you have to do is have breasts. That's what he said. "It doesn't matter if the woman is unwilling." The man's desire is so strong, his rights so undeniable, his desire overwhelms.

Billie and Billie 2: "That's why God made men bigger than women,"

Billie: he said. I hate that God.

He said I'd never enjoy sex because I don't want to lose control. He said you think you don't need a man. He said I should loosen up.

Relax. He couldn't wait. Big Wally took over.

I dreamt that I walk into his bedroom and I rip off the sheets. He lies there naked with his penis shrinking and whinnying like the melting witch in Oz. I silently stand around, watching it deflate emitting a steady stream of putrid green air. His ugly body and face melt. He turns into a cherry bomb. I light it in the house and run away while the stench kills flying bugs and insects instantly.

And you think the anger is yet unresolved. Yes, it is. How does it go away? How can it leave?

Billie 3: Affection. Such a dream I've had. My most wonderful lover comes home to me and slips into my bed on a Sunday morning.

Billie 2: The sunlight falls gently through the shade.

Billie: The mellow light hides the flaws of our bodies -- hides the exactness of the fat. No, I didn't mean fat. Well, I meant fat but not in my dream.

Billie and Billie 3: I dream my lover holds me in just the right way.

Billie 3: strokes my back, soothes my neck, and tells me life was meant to be like this.

Billie: My lover finds the scars on my abdomen and asks, without fear, where they came from.

Billie 3: I tell this kindly person the story for each and my past is accepted and gently pursued. More scars are found and addressed.

Billie: Falls and pencils and screwdrivers and knives. Ice and matches and ego. Closed hands and open fists.

Fear mends the wounds. Fear scars. Scars hide the wounds.

I can't get past the fear today. Sometimes it's OK. I lied. It's never OK. It makes me throw up. It's repulsive.

I faked the dream. It never was dreamt. I needed it so you would think I was normal sexually. It would have been easier that way. But, I can't feign pleasure. The words may be there. The intonation might be right but there is no memory of pleasure. I created the memory from reading too many books.

Billie 3: But I play my music and sometimes something magical happens.

Billie: Sometimes my arm doesn't hurt and my fingers aren't tired.

Billie 3: Sometimes I squeeze the note

Billie: right out of my left hand. The instrument vibrates

Billie 3: with a clean pom pom pom.

Billie and Billie 3: The harmonies become so intimate.

Billie: The pitches are exact

Billie 3: and ring so true --

Billie and Billie 3: wide open --

Billie 3: the heavens open and the note reverberates as if

Billie: it was pulled out of an instrument played in a large stairwell.

Billie and Billie 3: It's so clean and powerful.

Billie: A viola. The forgotten instrument of the orchestra. The instrument of untalented but wishful kings who demanded they be allowed to join in the kingdom's quartet. The instrument of off beats and simple harmonies.

Ah, but when it's taken seriously, when it's studied like a solo instrument, when it's played with

Billie 3: strength and tenderness, no instrument compares to its mellow, pensive tone.

Billie: skill, technique, and just the right intensity.

(Pause.)

Billie continues *(thoughtfully)*: I have a dream. I dream you come to me when I'm in pain.

Billie and Billie 3: You wipe away my tears

Billie 3: and smooth the hair away from my face. You, in your silly little way, have trouble moving the strand of hair that, somehow, got stuck in my mouth. You have trouble grabbing it. After you find it, it slips through your grasp, repeatedly.

Billie: Your acts of kindness, though awkward, amuse me.

Billie 2: I forget the pain.

Billie 3: When I smile, you lie on the bed next to me. You tell me you're a doctor as you peek beneath the sheets. I, trying not to laugh, say, "No. No doctor has spent this much time with me."

You take a gentle inventory of my body parts -- to make sure they are all there. You act as if it's all brand new -- as if this is the first time.

I expect you to tell me to breathe deep.

Billie: But I find I already am.

Billie and Billie 3: I shiver in an unsustainable gladness.

Billie: Your face is so beautiful. You cut your hair too short. It should be longer and more flowing to show off the gentleness you like to hide. No one else sees something in me to love, to protect.

> *(Offstage: the sound of someone pounding on a door or a body slamming into something.)*

Billie and Billie 3 *(to Billie 2)*: I want to hold you

Billie 3: to protect you.

Billie 2: From what? Why?

Billie: I can't say.

> *(Off-stage: Louder. Sound of someone pounding on a door or a body slamming into something.)*

Billie 3: You have to.

Billie: Oh, dear God! Oh, dear God.

Things start out OK but suddenly, they get violent. Like my line dream. Friendly lines get violent.

He touched me so gently, so softly. He wakes me up. Tells me to be quiet. "Don't wake anyone up," he says. For a long time, his body rests into mine, taking the cool off the evening and the clean sheets. He says he likes my nightgown -- says I look so grown up. He says his wife's in the hospital. She's been in there a long time. Too long for a man to go without love." He strokes my hair, gently moving it off my forehead. His hand moves to my face, then from my face to my neck to my breast. "All, such a big girl. Growing up. Pretty soon you'll be a young woman. A beautiful budding woman. No longer a little girl. A princess. A woman."

He asks me to play a game with him.

Billie 2: No, I'm tired. I have school tomorrow.

Billie: "Come on," he says. He kisses me and his lips linger too long. "All, princess." I am puzzled and frightened. He kisses me again. His tongue slips between his lips and pries mine apart. I feel what I think is a belt buckle but he isn't wearing pants. He always walks around the house in his underwear. We always notice the bulge in his shorts. His machine. His Big Wally. Hanging beneath the belly that hangs over the waistband.

I want you to know how I was thinking, how I was raised, so you don't blame me. I was young. I didn't know what he was doing. I only knew it probably wasn't right. I didn't like him to touch me this way but he was ... I didn't like his ...

His breath smells of coffee. His tongue still holds the taste of sugar. I figured this tongue thing was something adults do but I thought it repulsive. I wish my mother were home. She wouldn't have let this happen. I wish I could make noise and wake someone up but then I think I don't want anyone to catch me like this.

I start crying. "Big girls don't cry."

Billie 2: "Big girls don't cry. Big girls don't cry. Big girls ...

Billie: I feel something pressing on my leg. Something like a giant, firm sausage.

"Now," he says, "I'm going to teach you something. I'm going to show you what you aren't to let anyone else do to you. You save this special experience for me. It's so special you can't tell anyone else or it will be ruined and it won't ever be special again. You don't want that to happen, do you? You want me to be proud of you. You want me to be happy, don't you? You're almost a woman now. Make me happy. Big girls don't cry, princess."

He tries to pry my legs apart with his knees. I resist. He gets mad. His whole face changes. He becomes a wild man. His face gets red and mean and his eyes turn to pure hate. He says, "If that's the way you want it." He slaps me and gets out of the bed. He stomps out of the room.

I think it's all over. I cry, softly, trying not to make a sound that will make him angry.

I cry myself to sleep. I wake up as he lifts me out of bed.

"I'm sorry," he says. "I'm going to make it up to you." He still looks funny. I don't feel safe but the words are right.

He carries me down the stairs, through the living room, and into the basement. He carries me into the laundry room. He had moved a mattress from the spare bedroom downstairs on to the floor. The washer and dryer are going. Tennis shoes bounce and thud in the dryer making a tremendous noise. Especially in the middle of the night. But he always does strange things at strange times. Maybe he wants me to help him do the washing or freshen the mattress or something. I know I'm wishing.

I don't know if anyone was awake. I don't know if they were afraid or not. They didn't stop it so it must have been all right. They would have stopped it if it were wrong.

He sets me down and wedges a chair beneath the doorknob and turns around. His face turns to pure evil again. Unless you've seen that before, you won't know what I mean and I can't think of another way to describe it. Just pure evil. Hate.

I cry. He hits me. I fall backwards. "I'll give you something to cry about," he says. He gets a rag out of the rag box and comes towards me. "Come here." I move away. "I told you to come here." I know there is no sense in running. He is 6' 4" and weighs 350 pounds. He looks like a giant.

I know if I get him any madder, things will only get worse. I go to him. He grabs me and gags me. I don't know why. No one would have heard anything with the radio and the washer and dryer going. No one, even if they did hear something unusual, would have come to my aid. It's just too risky to get in his way when he's angry. Anyway, I was too scared to talk or scream.

His right hand lifts my face so I have to look at him. "Now, don't you ever put makeup on that pretty little face. And lipstick, if you ever use lipstick, I'll … I'll … Don't use lipstick; it takes the color right out of your lips. Promise me you'll never wear lipstick. I said premise me you'll never wear lipstick."

Billie 2: I'll never wear lipstick.

Billie: "Louder," he says.

Billie 2: "I'll never … I'll never …"

Billie: He slaps me.

Billie 2: never wear lipstick.

Billie: "That's a good girl."

"Now, when you get older, boys will want to take you out and they will want to do this." He raises my nightgown and gropes at my chest. I back up and back up until my back hits the wall. "Yes," he says squeezing my breasts, "boys will try to do this. See, they'll move their hands like this and press like this but you don't let them do that. Right?" I shake my head. "Right?"

Billie 2: Yes.

Billie: I mumble through the rag.

"Sometimes these bad boys will put their mouths on your chest like this and pretend they are drinking bottles in their mother's arms. And they'll suck and suck arid suck just like this. And what the boy wants you to do is to hold his head like this." He forces me to cradle his head in my right arm and drop my left arm down his back.

And he sucks and sucks and sucks. Then, he bites me and says, "I'm sorry," and begins rubbing the bite mark with his left hand. While he does that, he puts his mouth on the other side. I was backed up into the wall so hard, I thought, I was likely to go through it. He presses harder and harder and the tears roll down my cheeks and fall off my face and onto the nightgown wadded up around my throat. Some tears fall on my body and he licks them up. I start gagging. He takes the rag out of my mouth and yanks me over to the basin where I throw up.

"Here," he says, "lie down here until you feel better." He seems to be getting better. Maybe his game is over. He lies down right beside me and strokes my hair until I calm down a bit. He kisses me and says, "You taste like barf, you little slut," and slaps me again. I start crying. He holds my face and tells me to stop.

He lifts my nightgown as if he is going to take it off me but then he rips it off explaining why I don't need it. "There is more to your lesson, princess, and for the other part, this will only get in the way."

I wish I were dead. I wish he would just kill me and get it over with.

"Now see isn't this better. Now I can love you all over and nothing gets in the way. You're frightened but you shouldn't be frightened. Everyone does this. This is how babies get made. This is what happens. You might as well get used to it."

I struggle, get slapped, and cry. He pries my legs apart again.

"Now, you let me and no one else do this. Open your legs. Open," he says more firmly.

I think of the dentist trying to get my brother to open his mouth so he could get a filling. "Open," the dentist said. "Open. It's for your own good. Open."

He lies on top of me. His weight. I thought every bone in my body was breaking. Suddenly, the pain. Is too. Much. He says, "Get used to it baby! This is what men do." He jerks forward and back and forward and back. I pass out.

Yes. That was the first time.

My father.

(Billie turns to Billie 2.)

Oh, I'm so sorry.

> *(Billie 2 goes to Billie. They hug. They cry. Billies hold each other. Pause. This needs much time. Billie 2 moves away. Billie moves a hair the crosses Billie's 2*

faces away, looks at her, and hugs her again. Rocking.)

Billie: It's OK. You can cry now. It's OK to cry.

(Billies 1 and 2 cry.)

It's OK.

(Billie 2 slowly stops sobbing. All of the Billie's take a deep breath in unison. Pause.)

Billie: It's OK to cry. It's safe to cry now.

Billie 3: Yes. Now.

(Billie and Billie 3 look at each other; first, in shock, then, in understanding.)

Billie 2: Yeah, it felt good.

I'm not so scared anymore.

(Eventually, Billie 2, trying to cheer Billie up, gives Billie her stuffed dog. Billie recognizes it and hugs both Billie 2 and the dog, as if Billie 2 has given her a great gift. Pause.)

Billie: Me, too.

Billie 2 *(to Billie 3)*: Billie, I'm tired of crying.

Billie and Billie 3: Yes.

Billie 2: Is it over?

Billie 3: No.

Billie: No more, now.

(Pause.)

Billie 2 *(relieved, to Billie 3)*: Will you play me a fiddle tune? A happy one? You know, like ones you used to play?

Billie 3 *(looking over Billie 2 at Billie):* You know I'd love to play for you, but this one says music makes her feel too much. You'll have to ask her.

Billie 2: Will you play for me?

Billie *(to Billie 2):* I haven't played for a long time. A really long time.

Billie 3 *(gently):* It's like riding a bike.

Billie 2: like riding a bike ... please play.

Billie: Oh ... I don't even have my instrument any more.

Billie 3: Come on. The truth. You never did sell it like you said you would   you couldn't.

Billie 2: It's over there.

Billie *(starting to tease Billie 2):* Where?

> *(Billie 2 signals to Billie 3. Billie 3 brings it over to Billie and Billie 2.)*

Billie: Thank you.

> *(Billie opens the case. All Billies look at the viola.)*

Billie 2: I thought violas have four strings.

Billie: They usually do. But, I haven't played in a while.

> *(Billie takes the instrument out and taps around the seams.)*

I'm surprised the thing's in one piece.

Billie 3: Me too.

Billie 2: Good glue?

Billie *(pulling the Billies together, laughing)*: Good glue.

> *(Fade to black. When the stage is completely dark, a solo viola is heard.)*

Appendix: Resources
This play may trigger memories in the cast and/or audience. Here are some resources that may be helpful.

For immediate help, call the National Sexual Assault Hotline: 800.656.HOPE

Rape, Abuse & Incest National Network (RAINN) is an American, non-profit anti-sexual assault organization. RAINN can help you find local support groups. www.rainn.org

Books
The Courage to Heal: A Guide for Women Survivors of Child Sexual Abuse, 20th Anniversary Edition
by Ellen Bass and Laura Davis

Beginning to Heal (Revised Edition): A First Book for Men and Women Who Were Sexually Abused As Children
by Ellen Bass and Laura Davis

Victims No Longer: The Classic Guide for Men Recovering from Sexual Child Abuse
by Mike Lew

Secret Survivors: Uncovering Incest and Its Aftereffects in Women
by E. Sue Blume

http://www.bearingthroughit.org/ChecklistJuly2004.pdf

The Body Keeps the Score: Brain, Mind, and Body in the Healing of Trauma
by Bessel van der Kolk M.D. (Author)

The Deepest Well: Healing the Long-Term Effects of Childhood Adversity
by Nadine Burke Harris M.D.

The previous two books use research on Adverse Childhood Experiences (ACEs) done by Drs. Vincent Felitti and Robert Anda:
http://acestudy.org/the-ace-score.html

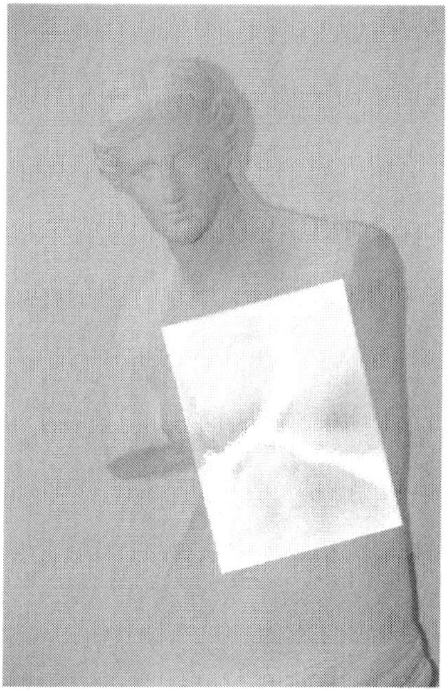

Made in the USA
Middletown, DE
22 July 2018